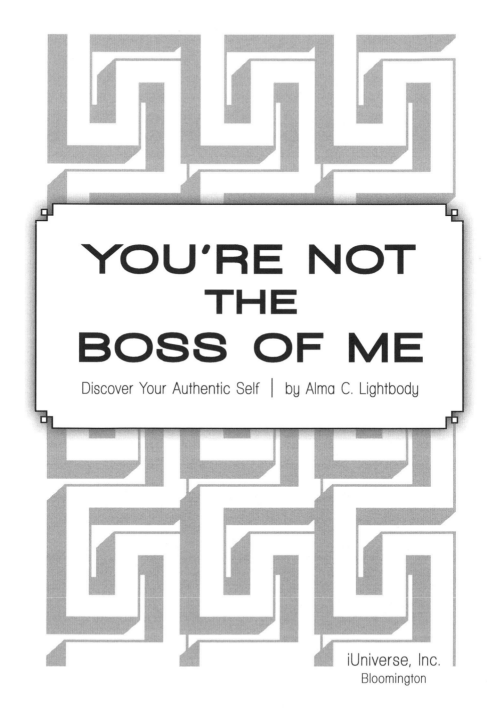

YOU'RE NOT THE BOSS OF ME

Discover Your Authentic Self | by Alma C. Lightbody

iUniverse, Inc.
Bloomington

You're Not the Boss of Me
Discover Your Authentic Self

iUniverse books may be ordered through booksellers or by contacting:

iUniverse
1663 Liberty Drive
Bloomington, IN 47403
www.iuniverse.com
1-800-Authors (1-800-288-4677)

ISBN: 978-1-4759-5037-3 (sc)
ISBN: 978-1-4759-5038-0 (hc)
ISBN: 978-1-4759-5039-7 (e)

Library of Congress Control Number: 2012917102

Printed in the United States of America

iUniverse rev. date: 10/29/2012

Contents

Preface

My interest in energy medicine began in 1990. It happened as a result of major changes in my life that made me realize the life I was living was false and could no longer sustain and support me. I wasn't in touch with my true inner self, and I was willing to do whatever it took to find the answer to the question, "Who am I?"

Like many others, I needed a catastrophe to make me wake up and look for what was hidden beneath the surface reality I had acquired and built in a pursuit of success. In my quest to create a new life, my curiosity in energy medicine led me through many modalities, teachers, mentors and experiences. Some key ones are:

Leyline Centre for Spiritual Practice: Michelle and Don Ley, 1 year

Healing Light Center Church: Rosalyn Bruyere, 5 years

Healing Touch International Certification: Janet Mentgen, 3 years

Principles of Hypnosis: Claire Etheridge, 2 years

Inca Medicine Wheel and Shaman Mastery Course: Mary Blankenship and Jose Luis Herrera, 6 years

Mentor, teacher and friend: Lois Ross, 20 years

During my training with these powerful teachers, the common thread was to release and shed what didn't serve me. I had to let go of excess baggage that did not belong to me in order to be a clear conduit of energy to help others. In my mission to understand more about myself, I found that helping and treating clients became a major part of my learning experience. I could see how the source of many people's problems was trying to live up to others' expectations and programming. The stress of these subliminal controls caused distress and disease.

I labelled these controls "bosses" and began to pay attention to where they came from and what effect they had on people's lives and personalities. These bosses have many faces and show up as patterns, imprints, family habits, opinions and much more. Not all of them are bad, but it is important to recognize what is true for you, and what is someone else's story. This search has been an interesting journey for many years, and my list of bosses has grown considerably.

Throughout my studies, similar controls were part of my clearing process. In an attempt to simplify years of work, I have singled out the bosses and want to share my concepts and instructions for an easier and faster way for everyone to understand. I have learned that once you become aware of where bosses come from and what influence they have on you, you have a choice to shed and release their control over you. You can take your life back, think your own thoughts, have your own opinions and in doing so be healthy and happy.

Do you care enough about yourself to delve into the mystery of who you truly are? You don't need special training, degrees or money to do the work—it is all about love for yourself. The journey is a simple, one-step-at-a-time adventure that only requires a commitment to uncover your authentic self and discover that *You Are the Boss of You.*

Introduction

Your picture of me is not authentic.
The picture you see is not me.
—Alma Lightbody

We've all heard young children declare, "You're not the boss of me," but somewhere along the line, they lose that determination and give in to the bosses of the world. They become pulled into the net of "should," "don't" and "can't" as the picture of their personality is painted by others. From the time they are born, they are imprinted with patterns and controls through the thoughts and agendas of parents, siblings, religion, race, culture, teachers and many other factors. They are brought up in a world that is programmed how to think, act, speak and respond. As they grow, the controls and webs get tighter and more restrictive because the powerful ego loves to be taunted by things such as material values, money, power, media and technology.

One day when something like trauma, grief, illness or depression blindsides us, we begin to question who we are and what life is all about. Such a thing happened to me when I was about forty-five years old. My relationship fell apart, and then a year later the company in which I was a partner went bankrupt. These shocks pushed me into a deep, dark hole before I began to question, "Who am I? Where do I go from here?"

I now would call that an awakening, but at the time I didn't recognize the blessing in the middle of my chaos. When I finally realized the gift I had been given, I thanked God and totally changed my life direction. I had no idea where I was going or how to get there, but I never looked back. As I began to look into a deeper side of myself, a whole new world opened up for me. To date, society had been responsible for my image, my education and my career, but now it could not sustain me; there was something missing. I could no longer hide behind the plastic mask I was wearing. I was not clear what got me to this point—I only knew it didn't feel good.

As I changed my way of looking at things, I became aware of the matrix of overlays and opinions of others that were smothering me and holding me hostage. I first noticed it in others and didn't realize I was looking at a mirror image of myself. My move into holistic health and energy medicine brought me more information. During treatment, when clients were in an altered state, they would reveal deep emotional wounds caused by the influence and control of others.

Over the years, my list of controls, bosses, imprints, patterns and influences has grown extensively, and the central core is always the same. The majority of the human race doesn't know who they truly are. They are sleepwalking through life, most often with someone else in control of their actions, thoughts and beliefs, telling them who they are and what they should do.

How do we speak up and be heard without breaking society's rules? How do we become a whole person with pieces being pulled from us in every direction? How do we keep our true personality separate yet still be integrated with others?

From the song "Amazing Grace," the words "I once was lost but now am found, was blind, but now I see" are totally different if you hear them literally rather than looking deeper into the spiritual meaning. It is time to look past the surface approach to life and find the contemplative, holistic one. Think of this concerning your life: What is it you don't see and are not in touch with?

The information in this book is offered to stir those latent childhood thought processes that fought the system with, "You're not the boss of me." It is meant to awaken possibilities long since buried. I include a few examples from my own experiences, but this is not my story—it is about you, so please look at it from your perspective. Take from it what speaks to you and works for you. *It's all about you.*

The level of consciousness in the world is speeding up, and as part of a collective universal community, it is our job to awaken, dig beneath the surface and locate the stories of how our personality developed. We need to take responsibility for our choices, find our own truth about what really matters to us and stand up for what we believe.

I was delighted when I recently read an article from a seniors' hospice. They'd just revised their concept of caring from control and drugs to freedom and choice. The rules have been relaxed, and their new motto is, "*We're not the boss of you.*" If an age-old childhood declaration has been heard, anything is possible.

This book offers a one-step-at-a-time opportunity to see your life from a new perspective. *Part 1* sets the stage with definitions and information about how influences from various stages in our lives imprint and mould our personality. As you move through this section, it will awaken an awareness of how such influences continue to affect your life. It will start your thought processes working, as you realize there is another person beneath the layers of illusion.

Part 2 is about how the body speaks to and communicates with you. In addition it helps you to understand the energetic and physical systems that support you. These systems provide valuable information about dysfunction and illness created by the programming in your life.

Part 3 takes work and commitment on your part as you play with the charts of possibilities. You will begin to realize there is more to you than you ever imagined. These are defining moments and worth all the time you spend on them. During this investigation, you will determine you have choice about what is your true personality and what is imposed and false.

Part 4 helps pull together what you have learned about yourself with supporting insights and stories. No two people are the same, so your journey into this awakened state is yours and yours alone. Your intuitive self will help you make friends with who you truly are and in what you believe. The world is changing and moving into a higher state of purity, love and peace. The unencumbered, genuine *you* whom you discover will be delighted to be part of this new beginning. The last pages are left blank for you to use for rewriting the story of who you are meant to be. Enjoy the journey—you'll love it!

PART I

Creating a Map of Your Belief System

ONE

Patterns, Imprints and Masks

The story of what happened to you while you were trying to find the path on your journey.
—Rosalyn Bruyere

WHAT HAPPENS WHEN YOU finally wake up and find you have been following someone else's dream? You've spent your life trying to please others and live up to their expectations, and in doing so you've lost your own voice. You begin to realize your personality is made up of the desires and controls of others. This chapter is the first step in understanding how your reality is birthed and controlled as you take your place in the world. You become part of planned agendas, and the resulting patterns, habits and imprints create expectations of who you *should* be.

A final destination of peace of mind and love is a motivating force to encourage you to create a map of your own belief system—a map of your *authentic self* that defines your truth and values as you know them.

The world is moving forward at a very rapid rate, as we can see by the constant progress of spirituality, technology and social media. When we talk about imprints from our childhood and schooling that need to be shed, it doesn't necessarily mean our parents and teachers were wrong or bad; some of their imprints and patterns are just outdated and are now excess baggage. These will be easier to shed than other deep emotional imprints, but with awareness and intent, we can break through all the illusions that control us.

We arrive at birth filled with an essence of innocence and purity, but through all the stages of our lives, others influence us as we take on numerous opinions, agendas, controls and bosses that are not us, but through time they are superimposed into our sense of reality and shape who we become. Some terms that are used to describe what we've become in our society are "living in a cultural trance" or "sleepwalking through life." They are about following the rules, doing what we are told is right and believing most of what we watch on television and read in newspapers.

A realistic example of how we are controlled came to me when I was talking to a friend about these thoughts. He said, "I know exactly what that is; I call it the 'hardly used' brain. First, my mom told me what to do, next my teachers told me what to do and then my wife told me what to do." We are constantly engulfed by people telling us what to do, how to think, what to say, how to dress, how to vote and so on. Even live theatres hold up signs for when we are supposed to applaud.

It is time to awaken to the changing dynamics in the universe right now. We all need to be present, grounded within ourselves and clear of our own direction. We need to learn about what masks we hide behind and how to remove them to find our original essence.

The following topics provide some basic information on various subjects that will come up throughout the book.

Patterns

The issues involved here are mainly to do with family, race, ancestry, religion, school and work. It's about the way things are done, such as procedures, habits, rules and beliefs. It's the conditioning we acquire from those around us on a routine basis. Within these patterns is how the family lives on a day-to-day basis, which includes habits around food, music, sports, educational values, TV, video games, where the parents work, relationships and the surrounding social environment. It also relates to what kind of atmosphere predominates in the home, be it loving, happy, violent, disconnected or any other option. The patterns create the initial programming in childhood and affect how we see things, hear things and, most of all, react to things. Patterns are repetitive in nature.

Imprints

This category is extensive and is still affected by family, but it also moves outside that nest to include grandparents, relatives, friends, teachers, mentors, coaches, ministers, role models and many others. While patterns have more to do with habits, imprints deal with things like honesty, secrets, truth, friendships, values and integrity. Imprints can deeply affect the forming personality and ego. An imprint can be a compliment that boosts self-esteem, or it can be a derogatory remark like "You are stupid," which has a destructive effect. All kinds of imprinting happen on a routine basis and are very critical in the developing years. If parents plan their children's careers and try to impose the desires they did or did not fulfill themselves, it can stop creative dreaming and limit possibilities.

Influences

These global bosses are very powerful and affect all of us as a collective consciousness, in some way. Some examples of influences are social technology, money, media, magazines and religion. The strong control of these powers is a major reason society lives in a cultural trance. We can walk away from influences more easily than ingrained imprints, if we choose not to trust or believe them.

Masks

Masks have been around throughout history; they are often used as a type of muse to hide one's identity. At a masquerade party, the mask is something we can physically see and touch and remove in an instant. A mask gives the perception we are someone other than ourselves, and we can wear all sorts of masks to keep changing the picture. In Shakespeare's original theatre, the actors played many roles and held up various masks to portray the different characters.

In our daily lives, we may not wear physical masks to change the perception of who we are, but symbolically we wear different masks of illusion all the time, and they change depending on the situation we are in. The big questions are: Why do we wear them? What do they cover up? Where do they come from?

Personality

The personality is about how you talk, walk, dress and present yourself to others. It is the cover you wear in your present life to influence how you want to be seen. The question is, do you present what you feel inside? The personality is strongly affected by ego.

Authentic Self

Your authentic self is your soul's compassion about honesty, truth, integrity, working from the heart, doing what you love and being clear about your opinions of life. It is wholeness. This quote from Andrew Cohen offers a good summary: "The authentic self is the best part of a human being. It's the part of you that already cares, that is already passionate about evolution. When your authentic self miraculously awakens and becomes stronger than the ego, then you will truly begin to make a difference in this world. You will literally enter into a partnership with the creative principle."

The Soul's Message

Occasionally, at our lowest level we might hear this inner voice saying, "I'm here, and I can help if you will listen to me. I will never overrule you, but if you pay attention to the ideas I conceive, then the mind will create, the body will take action and we will work as a team to bring you wholeness."

We all need to allow quiet time in our lives to be able to hear these subtle messages. The soul is timeless love and doesn't hold grudges; it is something no one else can ever take away from you, no matter what happens. It is ever faithful to you, your true, authentic self. It is always ready to help clear old baggage and make space for your genuine truths. Be willing to ask.

The Spoken Word

The formation of patterns and imprints are created through words, actions and the underlying energy around you. Words are a vow you make to yourself and others; they create thought images, and thoughts create reality. They are powerful teaching tools if we pay attention to what each word carries. If they are positive, inspiring and creative, they can move us forward and open doors of opportunity and growth. Other types of words can be diminutive, fearful and destructive. Scenarios are created in our mind with words such as "impossible," "can't," "limitation," "difficult" and "should," that can cause withdrawal or anger and repress possibilities of greatness. The way we speak to people as a parent, sibling, teacher or employer affects the self-esteem and personality of the recipient in some way.

Filters

"What I said is not what you heard." This statement is a reality for most of us because we all speak through filters we have developed regarding how we perceive things. Patterns and imprints from our life experiences create filters unique to each of us that affect how we see, judge and react to people and circumstances. We are unaware of how restrictive these filters can be and wonder why communication with others can be so difficult. Once we learn how to recognize their presence and acknowledge where they come from, we have an opportunity to release their effects.

False Gods

We create false gods through how we perceive their power over us. We believe they are better, have more authority and know more than we do. In our minds we place them on a pedestal, remain silent and allow them to tell us what to do. Some examples would be parents, doctors, employers, presidents and dictators.

The Onion Analogy

Removing imprints imposed on you by others can be likened to peeling away layers of an onion: it is best done slowly with intent, one layer at a time. If you peel the layers away all at once, it may be hard on you. Learn to lift the peels one by one, layer by layer, slowly and with care. Be respectful of your vulnerability and self-worth as you introduce yourself to your true self.

Power of Presence

Very few people are able to be in the present moment on a regular basis, even though it is a place of power. We carry values and assumptions from the past as heavy baggage and move them forward into the future. The past drains our energy, and dwelling on what might be in the future also takes away from the power of the present moment. We have a choice to stay in the present moment and recognize old issues and imprints for what they are.

One of my teachers, a Q'ero elder named Don Manuel Quispe, tells us, "Be aware; we have all adopted patterns during our journey—some hurtful, some just from the innocence of not knowing better but the past is history and needs to be released in order to give power to the presence and what we need now. The past issues are not important."

Creating a Story

We've talked about how opinions and the agendas of others influence us, but sometimes we can be our own worst enemy. The reality we live in is often a story we create in our mind that doesn't even happen. How often do you begin to think of an issue that's bothering you, and you find yourself creating a scenario of what you imagine someone might do or say? Even though it's all in your mind, you are upset with that person or issue; you are convinced it is real. An example is how in relationships, we tend to create a story in our mind of how we want someone to act and feel. When they don't live up to our expectations, we think they have failed us— even though they have no idea what the expectation is.

That's often how we create the stories in our life, and they are just that—stories. They are not us. If we hang on to the stories we've created, they suck the life out of us. Mind stories can be so powerful and convincing that they become internalized, as if they really happened; the resulting stress is the same.

Secrets and Lies

From the beginning of our lives, we are immersed in a maze of contradictions. What is shown in body language is often not what is spoken. From the time we are small, we are told secrets we are not supposed to share because it's a secret, sometimes a family secret and other times our own. In more severe cases they are secrets of trauma and abuse that become locked inside.

In school we might tell and share secrets about others, some real and some fictitious. When we can't remember whom we told secrets to, we begin to lie to cover up the secrets, and then we lie to cover up the lie. The cycle goes on, and years later we find ourselves in therapy, trying to unwind these interwoven cycles of confusion. We might call these family habits, but sometimes we create a reality of self-inflicted stress for which we have to take responsibility.

Speaking Our Truth

This is a sensitive topic that is often misunderstood. The surface truth is about being honest in your words and actions when dealing with others, as well as yourself. Then there is speaking your truth about your feelings and more sensitive issues. In this case sometimes saying what others want to hear is easier, so we tend to take the road of least resistance.

In my journey I found learning to speak the truth was not as easy as trying to learn a sport. I needed to experience aspects of truth in myself to be aware of its meaning. During a time of major life changes, I received some guidance from a woman who channelled Archangel Michael. Part of the advice I was given was to *speak my truth*.

This advice mystified me for many years following that reading; it didn't resonate with the surface or literal world I was living in. I thought I was truthful; I wasn't a liar. If someone gave me too much change, I would give it back. I didn't cheat on my taxes. I felt I was an honest person, but later I began to realize all that was small potatoes in the grand scheme of things. The *truth* I was looking for was much deeper.

I didn't even know my own truth, so how could I speak it, act it or walk the walk? I didn't know the truth as my soul did. My life was clouded with imprints and veils of deception of which I was not even aware.

It is not common for society to teach us how to get in

touch with that inner part of us, the deep, spiritual self. We see the diagrams of the equilateral triangle for mind, body and soul, but in reality our society mainly focuses on the mind (business) and the body (vogue images), while the soul is barely given honourable mention.

Since my channelling 20 years ago, with the message to speak my truth, I finally get it. It's been an enlightening but cumbersome journey as I peeled back layers of my onion. It doesn't have to be difficult or take that long anymore. The steps in this book are meant to lighten your load and speed up the process of finding your truth, your authentic self.

Freedom

Freedom exists when you are free of patterns, controls and imprints imposed by others' agendas. It will take awareness, time and acknowledgement to keep bringing you back to your goal of freedom, because imprints are well embedded as unconscious habits. You must train yourself to recognize and respond when you slip back into them; it's a job. There will be some influences you choose to honour because it feels right. In that case, freedom exists because it is your choice.

Two
Awareness

*Most of us don't know ourselves well
enough to know what we want.*
—Shirley MacLaine

Now that you have a sense of the book's focus and its
related terms and topics, it is time to take the next step. This
chapter will help you understand at what point in your life
imprints were most likely to be embedded, and what other
worldly influences played a role. It's a good time for you to
get involved and pay attention to what influences have a hold
on you.

When I began this book, I focused on a few obvious
categories that affect us all, as a collective consciousness.
As I delved further into this idea of bosses and spoke to
more people, I realized the list was never ending. The
controls weren't just from people, feelings, institutions and
technology but from something much deeper that goes
back through generations of race, religion, genetics and
traditions; also included are the current stresses of our
changing world. Some influences may seem like natural
guidelines for safe and healthy living, and others are more

binding. Who is to say how these bosses affect any one of us? Our life experiences are not the same, so we see things through different filters, and what controls one person may be a non-issue for someone else.

This section provides examples of possible imprints and controls that painted the picture of your life. These are my own opinions, and each reader will relate to different parts of them. This stage of exploration is just meant to be thought provoking as you start to think about your history of issues, experiences and landmarks that have built your life into who you are today. You live through numerous stories about what you should do; some are exciting and pointed you in the direction of your dream, while others are orders given and commitments made in your best interest. If they made you uncomfortable or unhappy, and you were forced to participate, they most likely are not you. These are the ones you want to pay attention to now.

The topics explored are meant to help you peruse possibilities in your mind as you begin to get a sense of how powerful and life-forming (or limiting) imprints and false gods can be. Words create images, so open your mind as you read through these examples regarding where imprints come from. You'll begin to remember other experiences that affect you and hold you back, so make a note of them and pay attention to the impact and feelings associated with them. Each issue you read about and add to your list will help spark your thought processes. Let things perk and flow through you as you begin to unveil hidden parts of your personality.

It is our job, as part of a collective universal community, to awaken, dig beneath the surface and locate the stories of how our personality developed. With clear thought and understanding, we will discover the truth of who we were meant to be. In the past we listened to other people's opinions and beliefs, and we made them our own. We were trained that way, but it's the lazy man's way.

Step up to the plate and take responsibility for your own choices. Find your truth about what really matters to you and become aware of how you honestly feel about an issue. You may get shunned by some who hold a different belief, but if that's the way they act—they are not friends but controllers. Make plans to know and speak your truth, and in that you will find selfless freedom.

There are major changes happening in our world and the universe as we move to a higher level of consciousness. Older systems of finance and authoritarian control are breaking down, and for a while chaos may be part of our evolution. We need to be clear about who we are so we can work together and compliment each other's strengths. One of my teachers, Rosalyn Bruyere, taught us about the ancient Egyptian mystery schools of enlightenment where the students spent a lifetime learning about the mystery of "who you are" and "who you are not." Time and technology have sped up, and we have an opportunity to awaken and move forward more quickly than they did and help our children do the same.

By the time you get to the next step on acknowledgement, you will have some ideas beginning to percolate in your mind that you will need to look into more closely. Once you acknowledge what controls you, you put yourself in a position of power with an opportunity to change. There is no perfect time to heal, there is just now, so let's get started.

FAMILIAL INFLUENCES AND CONTROLS

Conception

A new life is planned from a soul's choice to return to earth, and from there the journey begins. Conception can be loving, stressful or sometimes violent. The time in the womb can be beautiful if the child is wanted, or it can be uncomfortable if the pregnancy is difficult and the parents are fighting. Parents' surroundings, diet, race and culture all have an affect on the pregnancy.

From a cozy and warm womb, the baby is pushed into the world, sometimes traumatically, and is surrounded by masked people and bright lights. The imprints have begun. It's impossible for a newborn to navigate this new journey without help, so from the very beginning it is influenced and controlled by the agendas of others.

In the grand scheme of things, others are the boss of us from conception onwards as we attempt to find our way through life. Our silent soul yearns for unconditional love with no strings attached, but often love, as it is perceived in our society, can be a major controller. In our learned expectation, it is something we need from someone else, and we spend much of our lives trying to earn love through someone else's approval.

Childhood

Initially children need food, shelter, security and nurturing, along with valuable and needed guidelines. Somewhere there is a balance—hopefully an intuitive and loving one, not a violent and abusive one. There is a sense of wonder and curiosity as children perceive new things and as the forming personality, frustration and ego become involved. Children are taught what is proper and appropriate, and these points of view are incorporated into their self-image. Parents, siblings, relatives and sometimes religion have the greatest influences on their life skills.

Included in all this are family dynamics. The early identity of the role of self within the family carries strong conditioning, whether spoken or unspoken. Children are taught what they are supposed to do. In the early years, social and environmental conditioning is run by the subconscious through imitating actions (e.g., monkey see, monkey do). During this time, family patterns and imposed imprints influence children's personalities. Impressions at this time are the biggest because kids are physically and mentally smaller than their bosses.

One of the most valuable teachings parents can offer is integrity. If the parents routinely honour a high sense of values, the children will follow what they see, feel and hear. If parents speak and act with a forked tongue, integrity is lost, and that leaves children bouncing from pillar to post trying to find some solid ground. When examples are poor, children can be sent heading in the wrong direction at an early age.

As the personality and ego continue to develop, children are like a sponge, taking in everything new and different, so they need high-quality examples and guidelines to protect them and teach them. A valuable tool needed in today's society is one of boundaries, which protects personal and sacred space. Children need to have an awareness of such protection and how to handle it, so that they are not led in the wrong direction by a possible predator.

School Years

For youth this is a time of creative fire and adventure: there are new beginnings and a new set of rules to follow. Unfortunately in the early school years, fantasy is controlled so that children will conform, and this continues the rest of their lives in various ways. Children are born with extraordinary creativity, but once they start getting programmed, they learn the rules of ordinary perception. They are part of a group trance, moving from grade to grade with a preset agenda. I love this quote from the children's book by Eric Blank[1] titled *The Success of Robert Fitzgibbons:* "I'd live in a world that I'd want to see, where people are friendly and choices are free. And no one would tell me what I'm supposed to be."

After grade school, hormones and physical image play a key role. There are more opportunities and choices available to try different things, and it's also a time for some wildness and rebellion. Teachers, technology, society, sports and competition impose new imprints, influences and rules. The presence of drugs, bullies and gangs suck in those yearning for inclusion and belonging. During these years there are a multitude of bosses that have an impact on values, integrity, confidence, direction and many more aspects of life.

Adulthood

Upon arriving at this stage of life, individuals are likely to be more experienced, trustworthy and responsible. We are talking in generalities here, but careers, relationships, marriage, travel and ego are key forces at this time of life. A cold and driven power to get ahead is dominated by money,

---

1   Blank, Eric. The Success of Robert Fitzgibbons: Las Vegas, Clark Morgan Press, 2007

media, vogue images and international communication. This technological age has a major level of control on just about everyone. Young adults are often living in a trance and waste energy to avoid feelings rather than deal with them. This is the time they need to awaken, being mature enough to know they don't know who they truly are, yet young enough that it can still make difference in the prime of their lives. I hope many in that group are reading this book.

Parenting

Controls are still very money oriented, but now they are partly as protector and provider. Parents' hearts open to the young lives for which they are responsible. The roles reverse a little as the children are bosses of the parents' time. The stress levels are high and the outside influences are great as parents juggle money, family and career. Time is in constant demand, and there is little time for personal needs. Keeping up with the Joneses is a major influence as well.

Empty Nesters

This is a very crucial time in life because so much energy has been put into career and rearing a family that all of a sudden the emptiness, both of the house and the heart, can be overwhelming and devastating. In some cases the provisional shell partners created to keep them together widens or falls apart, and divorce ensues. Other symptoms can be depression and a sense of uselessness.

The years of school, work and family have kept people so busy that they haven't had time to even think about who they truly are. Finally the nest is empty, work is not fulfilling and they have a big empty space inside of them.

What do they do with that emptiness? Pills can cover up the depression for a while, but they can't fill that vacant feeling that makes one feel crazy. People begin to question what life is really all about. Men tend to keep busy with golf, sports or other toys, and they don't take time to think about the emptiness; they don't connect with the emotional centre the way women do, so they don't feel the same sense of loss. Women yearn to be connected with something deeper. The big question of "Who am I?" arrives after all these years of busyness, as well as "Now what?"

Buried under imprints, controls and masks, with the label of mother and father gone, there is a mystery about what happened. It is important to understand this phase of life and question why it took so long to search for the silent soul, waiting to be heard.

Ageing Parents

Life has come full circle, and in some cases the adult children are responsible for their ageing parents. The parents have control of their children's time, but the children are now the boss of them. At this age ego no longer drives the experience, and elders are more themselves than ever before. With the innocence of a child, they are sometimes more honest and authentic, and suffer no more lies about what life holds.

My advice to everyone is not to wait until you are this age to find your true self. Start peeling off the layers of the onion now, and enjoy who you are meant to be much earlier in life.

WORLDLY INFLUENCES AND CONTROLS

The topics in this section are listed alphabetically, not by any sense of priority.

Communication

Communication is a basic skill and is an important need for all of us. The discussion here is about personal, real-life communication between people who are physically present. "What I said is not what you heard," and "What you said is not what I heard." Understanding each other includes hearing, seeing, listening, speaking, body language and a sense of the surrounding energy. We tend just to focus on the words and don't pay attention to the other elements that create the whole picture.

> We all have imprints and filters that we perceive things through, and the person we are talking to has a different set of perceptions.

> We most often don't completely listen to what someone is saying because we are already thinking of our response, which includes our own example of the story being told.

> We often are not speaking our truth but are instead saying what we think the person *wants* to hear, or what we think we *should* say.

> We pay little attention to body language, which is a clue to whether what is coming out of others' mouths is what they truly feel and mean.

Communication through conversation is based on: 7 percent words, 23 percent tone of voice, 35 percent facial expression and 35 percent body language.[2]

The communication through texting, e-mail and social media misses most of these attributes, and the warm, fuzzy feeling of personal communication is lost. Technology uses mainly words and sometimes pictures. A good example of this comes from a newspaper article by Vito Pilieci for *Postmedia News*, quoting a clinical psychology student Marisa Murray, who was having lunch in a restaurant. She found herself paying attention to people at a table beside her, where a family was socializing—but not with each other. Everyone from kids to grandparents were nose deep in an electronic device. "It was so strange. There was no conversation. Within the family, everyone had a cell phone. They ordered their appetizers and then all got back to their device. There was minimal conversation among the family."

As we continue through various topics, you'll understand how many exchanges would work better if we really understood what each other meant. Telepathy in days of old was much simpler because it was just about reading each other's mind—direct, clear and totally honest. When our words and actions are in harmony, wisdom and authenticity emerge.

---

2   I have carried this piece of information around for years but did not keep the reference. The closest I can find is on a website for westsidetoastmasters.com: "Albert Mehrabian, a pioneer researcher of body language in the 1950s found that the total impact of a message is about 7 percent verbal (words only) and 38 percent vocal (including tone of voice, inflection and other sounds) and 55 percent non-verbal."

Ego—Small Word, Big Boss

Ego is a driver, a self-inflicted injury to our being and a major control factor in our lives. If we are attached to it, we feel a constant demand on our being. The ego will fight with all its might to hang onto its detail-oriented, manufactured reality. Ego goals do not have our best interests at heart, because ego is not us. Yet ego is responsible for how we look, act and present ourselves to the world.

The word "should" is the taskmaster of ego and tells us all the things we have to do to look good, get good grades, make money and prepare for heaven. It's all about how we are seen in the eyes of others. If we stop identifying with ego, a weight dissolves. Even though the ego is part of our personality, we do have control over who is in charge. We have choice and control over everything we do. When we allow our heart and love to take precedence over the ego, we will come from a place of peace and joy. By buying into ego identities, we create a false reality that drains us, disorients us and sucks the core out of our being. Think about where the ego sits in the hierarchy of your life.

To liberate yourself you must decide you are interested in
bustin' loose from the mental habit of enslavement to the ego.
—Jennifer Hadley

Medical Systems

As we go through life, it's important to take charge of ourselves, but we often give that control to others—sometimes unwillingly, sometimes unknowingly, but often because we want someone else to deal with the problem and "fix" us when something goes wrong. For a long time we have had such expectations of the medical profession: we want them to make us better while we remain impassive and expect them to do all the work.

In the past, most people allowed doctors to control what happened to them without becoming involved, but in the last few decades many have begun to explore complementary health care options. The idea that medical science alone has all the answers to healthy living is no longer accepted as valid. Though the value of mainstream medicine remains, its practices are often dealt with through the Band-Aid approach, using drugs or surgery for a quick fix instead of looking for the deeper source of the problem.

The use of complementary therapy is a key addition to the healing process; it's a step towards people speaking up and being involved so they become the boss of themselves. The use of such therapies is not an "either/or" situation with conventional medicine but a team effort. The difference is that the patient can be the captain of the team, be fully involved and work with everyone to make informed choices. When you as a patient become involved and make a decision to heal, you have reached a place of empowerment. The power of the mind, body and soul work together to make a difference in the healing process; this may include lifestyle changes, diet changes and homework to find what is important to your body, but at least you have used your voice and have become involved.

Media, Newspapers and Magazines

In a world full of controls, our brains are hijacked by a barrage of opinions and the will of others. We need to know enough to tell the difference between truth and lies. The media is strongly influenced by government, the very rich and large corporate sponsors that feed us what they want us to hear and what serves them best. Their controls and tentacles run deep into the heart of our society and as the powerful money mongers of the world, they are referred to as the elite. Many people worldwide believe the media exclusively and have no discernment that they are being fed only what they are supposed to hear. Most often the collective population is not willing to step up and question what they are being told. They have become lemmings that follow a group consciousness planned for us by others.

I found this quote in *The Four Insights*, by Alberto Villoldo, and the issue is still the same after all these years. "As far back as 1880, John Swinton, a writer at the *New York Times* was quoted as saying, 'the business of journalists is to destroy the truth ... we are the tools and vessels of the rich men, behind the scenes.'" This ongoing conditioning of our consciousness can cause fear, hate and numbness in an instant, as well as strongly affect elections, the money market and wars. Such distractions are created to cover up parts of the truth and play with our emotions.

Magazines with movie star and vogue images are a huge venue used to control our younger generation, especially females. Advertising the female body creates the image that it is a business, a fiesta; it sets a standard for how you should look, dress and act, as well as what you should wish for in a relationship. The follow-up from this is diets, bulimia, anorexia, implants and plastic surgery in an attempt to be the perfect person. Such a plastic creation is really a person smitten by an image of someone else's thought forms. What a teacher of mine, Lisa Summerholt, said about identity is, "If you let others define or decide if you're smart or beautiful, you are giving your power away. Don't let others opinions define you." Seeking the approval of others abandons our true nature.

Television, computers, e-mails, texting, video games and social media now dominate most households. We need to evaluate the impact of imprinting ourselves with so much violence on TV. Before TV and mass communication, we experienced violence rarely; now we watch violence every day.

The overwhelming, addictive nature of the Internet may offer us tons of information, but it also stifles creativity and limits the quiet time for which the soul longs. The social media and Google have their places, but like anything else that is excessive in nature, it can hold people captive. Years from now I envision that we'll all have turned into robots with carpal tunnel in our thumbs from texting.

Money Power

Money is a thing, not a person, but it definitely controls the masses. It seems to control everything we do: food, shelter, clothes, image, travel, sports, work, investment and more. We let it control us, we honour it, we worship it and we are jealous of others who have more than we do. In the last few decades, the credit card enslavement has increased money's control of us exponentially. Due to a lack of attention to the fact that credit cards are not a bottomless pit of money, many are caught up in a life-binding debt compounded by high interest rates. Most of it happens as people become more addicted to material values. Many of the current generation have been brought up with credit cards in their pockets, and they have a poor respect for the true value of money. Even the government has some control over us, through taxation, to satisfy their needs for spending.

At the pinnacle of our society, the elite work to control the collective by keeping them ignorant and fearful. It is up to us to recognize their overbearing control and break free from their social programming. As we awaken and take our power back en masse, we become a formidable opponent to their control. In their own way Egypt did just that: they demanded the dictatorship stop and it happened. The recent Occupy Wall Street movement in many countries is a great start as people demand to be heard. This action is positive, nonviolent and speaks for all of us. We have more power than we give ourselves credit for—if we use it wisely.

Relationships

This is a huge topic because we have many different types of relationships throughout our lives. I will use spousal relationships as an example, but most issues involved here will also relate to the other types of relationships.

What you have read so far brings to light the controls, patterns and influences that shape your personality. If the identity created for you is not real, it is difficult to show your true self to others because you don't know who you are. With this confusion, how can you know what you want in a relationship?

Considering we don't understand this underlying mystery when we enter into a relationship, the following offers some advice that can help us learn about more aspects of ourselves. A relationship is a journey we experience with someone else; it is an active mirror reflection of who we are and who we are not. The partner reflects back to us what we need to learn about ourselves. This is a powerful concept to absorb, but it has significant meaning in many parts of our lives. It is important to cast out cynicism and blame so we can acknowledge and be thankful for what we are being taught. We have lessons to learn about ourselves—if we can become an observer and not take things personally.

The early parts of a relationship are often masked by romance and sex, which cover up the personality even further. When this glow diminishes and reality sets in with day-to-day life, we may find we are no longer on the same wavelength. The unknowingness of each other's true self throws a bag of mixed messages into the pot, and genuine communication is very difficult. The divorce rate in our society is extremely high, and it's easy to see why.

A relationship is always a work in progress, and it needs nurturing and understanding on an ongoing basis with each partner having an equal footing. If one partner is weaker, the relationship becomes one of attachment or codependence; the stronger partner is the boss of the other. As an example, in a workshop I was in with Rosalyn Bruyere, she talked about the Marriage Basket Syndrome. It is about a person who can't be alone so moves from one marriage basket to the next with no thought of individuality or a sense of self. This is also common in an abusive relationship, when someone continues to follow similar violent energy patterns because they don't know how to look after themselves and being alone requires change or stepping into an unknown void.

The Dali Lama's advice is, "Remember, the best relationship is one in which love for each other exceeds the need for each other."

Religion

This is one of those sticky categories that people don't really like to discuss. Like politics, it's a place even angels fear to tread. Religion is the holy controller of each of us, whether we admit it or not. Each religion feels it has the best take on how we evolved and who's the boss of our universe.

When I first began searching for my inner truth 20 years ago, I read some of Shirley MacLaine's books. She was on the same journey as I was and shared her powerful and fun life experiences in her writing. I related to her thoughts on a number of issues and religion is one of them. The following are words from a teacher in her book *Out on a Limb*: "Your religions teach religion—not spirituality. Religion has exploited man for the most part. Your world religions are on the right track basically, but they do *not* teach that every individual is fundamentally the creator and controller of his own destiny."[3]

At least, from what I can tell, there is a common sense of love as the core of all religions. Unfortunately in most, it doesn't receive the highest rating on the charts. Religion has been the basis for wars and killing throughout time. Control and money, along with the fear of hell and damnation, have a higher priority than love. The al Qaeda regime brainwashes young men into believing suicide bombing is God's will and the road to Nirvana. Catholicism is the richest entity in the world and preaches hell and damnation if one doesn't follow their rules; they believe in a Virgin Mary and a celibate Jesus, which gives the impression that sex is a sin. Buddhists, who focus on the spiritual self, spend time saving all things great and small and are definitely clear that love is the answer. Hebrews have been forsaken and abused throughout history, but they hold on to the belief they are the chosen ones, and they hold family, community and love high on their list.

---

3   Shirley MacLaine. *Out on a Limb*, New York: Bantam Books, 1983.

Within these various scenarios, each religion has its own way of worshipping God. Over the centuries they have developed and followed rituals, procedures and dogma that control their devotees and followers.

New agers believe God is within all of us and that peace, love, harmony and oneness are the template for the new, higher level of consciousness. Atheists don't believe in God but are subliminally infused with curiosity and confusion for not believing in anything. Then we have the pseudo-religions such as cults, where the control comes from the main man with God as a cover. Jehovah's Witnesses and Mormons are communities with fear-based rules and controls. These are only a few samples of how religion and its belief system control many of us subliminally or overtly. It is a major boss of this world and a difficult one for many of us to let go of for fear of reprisal. It is one of the deepest imprints.

Religion is a good topic to focus on and see how it relates to you. Listen to your intuitive, gut sense. If religion drains you, controls you or creates fear, then you need to pay attention to whether these beliefs are yours or something imposed on you. On the other hand, if it feeds you and makes you feel good, then it's surely something you made a decision about for yourself.

Social Role Expectation

I recently watched a movie about a college created in 1954. Women were trained to get married and look after their husbands; they were taught to cook, set tables, clean, dress appropriately and have a drink waiting for their husbands when they arrived home from work. This college was a new concept for females, so they could add a college degree to their title of wife. The expectation was to create perfect families (whatever their definition of perfect was). It was a major control issue of collective programming for what some elite group decided was the right thing to do. Genetic links and family imprints of this type still flow through us to a certain degree.

How we dress, what clubs we belong to, what social functions we are invited to, where we holiday and what schools our children are accepted into are part of a societal role that provides some kind of status. It most often has to do with money, and it can cause severe stress when not attainable. Ego is totally involved in this picture, more so than happiness. Social roles that seek validation and social position are assimilated into collective fantasies and do not support the soul's agenda.

A good way to handle these expectations is to think about this quote. "It's none of my business what other people think of me." It's been around so long I have no idea where it came from, but I love it.

Work, Employers and Coworkers

This topic involves our livelihood and consumes a major portion of our waking hours as well as our focus. The business we work in could be a large corporation or a small, self-owned business, but the people dynamics are similar. People we work with or for most often have a different perspective on the way they see things, and within that are a multitude of personal agendas. Think about how relationships look at things through different filters; in some ways, work is also a type of relationship. Our varied backgrounds create different opinions and can cause problems with communication that include such things as competition, secrets, gossip, occlusion and sometimes bullying. In addition, within the workplace environment are procedures, rules and actions to which we need to adhere. Some people rise to the top and take control, while others just do what they are told. If we don't speak up for ourselves, this is the point when we need to look at childhood imprints and patterns that imply we are not good enough, we don't count.

With that being said, work is often an enjoyable place, and the job still gets done. It is important to be aware that none of the above issues should ever degrade our integrity and values. If the job sparks creativity and productivity, it is a good place to be. Even if the job is routine, no matter how small, we can still work with enthusiasm to do the best job we can and be proud of what we achieve.

If your situation makes you unhappy, you do have choices. You can leave, or you can be bigger than the surrounding pettiness and not take things personally. Rather than having someone or something control your feelings, you can set the stage for the way you want to be treated by doing onto others as you would have them do unto you. With that simple action, you've made the first step towards a healthy work environment for yourself and others.

THE NEXT STEP

By now you've begun to realize there is more to you than you knew about. After looking into where possible superimposed imprints and patterns come from, you are getting the sense of who you are not. As you move forward, it's important to make your newly discovered information meaningful for you without blame or judgment for yourself or others. It is now your job to decide what is true for you and what you want to let go of. If any of these issues caused you trauma, then forgive and leave the past behind. It may take time, but forgiveness offers you freedom to move forward. Forgiveness for any misplaced or unintentional imprint or pattern can only be of value.

As you take responsibility for your life, the next step is to make friends with the true self or soul that dwells deep within your heart. How do you go about that? It is pretty easy; you just have to

- shed what doesn't serve you;
- speak your truth;
- think with your heart;
- don't take things personally; and
- put your ego in your back pocket.

The words look simple; you'll need lightness and humour if you want to enjoy new ways to look at life. It is time to play.

When you choose to find your true, unmasked self, the next two sections will help you with your adventure. You will find part of your old life disappearing as new beginnings appear. The reward will be powerful, enlightening and very worthwhile. Celebrate your successes. There will be no bands playing, but you will feel it in your heart—you'll just love it!

A long-standing Hopi prophecy seems very fitting for the work you are doing, for yourself and for the universe as a whole. Read it carefully and pay attention to how the symbology relates to you.

Hopi Prophecy

You have been telling the people that it is the eleventh hour ... now you must go back and tell the people this is *the hour.*

And there are things to be considered ...

Where are you living?
What are you doing?
What are your relationships?
Are you in the right relation?
Where is your water?
Know your garden.
It is time to speak your truth.
Create your community.
Be good to each other.
And do not look outside yourself for the leader.

Then he clasped his hands together, smiled and said, "This could be a good time! There is a river flowing now very fast. It is so great and swift that there are those who will be afraid. They will try to hold on to the shore. They will feel they are being torn apart and will suffer greatly. Know the river has its destination. The elders say we must let go of the shore, push off into the middle of the river, keep our eyes open, and our heads above water. And I say, see who is in there with you and celebrate.

At this time in history, we are to take nothing personally. Least of all, ourselves. For the moment that we do, our spiritual growth and journey comes to a halt.

The time of the lone wolf is over. Gather yourselves! Vanish the word "struggle" from your attitude and your vocabulary. All that we do now must be done in a sacred manner and in celebration.

We are the ones we've been waiting for.

PART II

The Body Speaks

THREE

Listening to Body Messages

*The physical body is the means our higher
level of consciousness has to communicate
with our personality consciousness.*
—Marlo Morgan, *Mutant Message*

THIS CHAPTER IS TUCKED between steps one and two and brings to light valuable tools you can use in your investigation. Our body is one of our best teachers in life if we honour its power and listen to its messages. It is like a storybook that communicates with us on a constant basis. Most of us know very little about how our physical bodies work externally, internally and especially energetically. Our body is a temple that houses an intricate map of systems working together to keep us alive and well. Also integrated within this complex life form is the anatomy of our soul, an energetic ball of light that carries the blueprint of our lives. In this section we will take a simplified look at how these systems work together and specifically how they speak to our personality consciousness through symbology. As you continue through this book and discover more about the imprints and influences that control your life, you will also realize how many of them have affected your health. This energetic summary is meant to help you understand the messages and warnings your body conveys to you.

Our Energy Body

Our bodies, like everything else in the world, are made up of energy, but what you see is the physical appearance. This structure is made up of a skeleton filled with several organs, glands, a brain and nervous system, a lymphatic system, a blood system with a heart that pumps blood through our body and lungs that breathe air in and out. Mixed in and around these structures and systems are muscle, tissue, ligaments and valves all enclosed by skin and hair. All of these parts are physical, and we are able to see and touch them.

The energy body or light body flows through and around our physical body. It can only be seen by a few people who have extended their perception, but it can be felt by most of us in one way or another. Pictures of this energy system of the body have been found on cave walls and structures going back thousands and thousands of years. The drawings are universally consistent, depicting seven circles aligned from tailbone to crown. They are recognized in the sacred teachings of both Eastern and Western medicine.

These circles, called chakras, are our body's energy centres and are associated with the colours of the rainbow. The energetic colour from each chakra radiates out into what is called the auric field, which extends an arm's length around the body. In a perfectly healthy state, when the chakras glow with their original radiance, this field is called the rainbow body. When the body is not cared for, the chakras become dull, blocked and sluggish, and illness can infiltrate our systems.

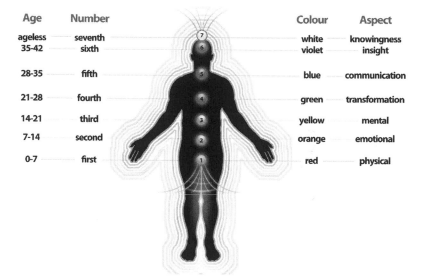

Age	Number		Colour	Aspect
ageless	seventh		white	knowingness
35-42	sixth		violet	insight
28-35	fifth		blue	communication
21-28	fourth		green	transformation
14-21	third		yellow	mental
7-14	second		orange	emotional
0-7	first		red	physical

FIGURE 1: CHAKRA POSITIONS AND THE AURIC FIELD

Each chakra has about a six-inch diameter and is a vortex of energy spinning clockwise and extending a few inches outside the body, both front and back. Connected above and below to each other just in front of the spine, they are a map of your inner world—your relationship to yourself and how you experience energy in your body.

Based on the location of each chakra in the body, they are connected with specific endocrine glands and govern associated organs close to them. These chakras, being connected with the auric field, inform and download information to the central nervous system and the glands to which they are related. There is a constant communication throughout your body.

Energy Centre Characteristics

The diagram in Figure 1 is further explained under the heading of each chakra. This information for the chakras is very basic in nature and is definitely not the total picture. It is meant to provide a template for the personality of each chakra and at what life stage various imprints and controls may have come into being, so you can track them more easily. The age of development varies with some teachers, but for simplicity I have used a common seven years between each chakra.

First Chakra

The colour is red, the age is 0–7 and it is located at the base of the spine. It governs understanding of the physical and is the centre through which one experiences fight-or-flight feelings. It is associated with the adrenal glands and governs the kidneys and spinal column.

This chakra is our connection to the earth, and its job is food, shelter and protection. Its focus is the need to be cared for. The biggest imprints are from parents, siblings, race, religion, language and, more recently, TV and video games. Early on, the child may have spiritual connections to the earth, may see auras and may have invisible friends.

Second Chakra

The colour is orange, the age is 7–14 and it is located a few inches below the belly button. It governs emotions, relationships and creativity and is associated with sexual glands, the prostate in males and the ovaries in females.

This is the age when hormones start to have influence and emotions create havoc. These newfound feelings can cause indulgence and addictions. There is a need to feel attractive and to draw others to you. The biggest influences are teachers, school friends and movie star images.

Third Chakra

The colour is yellow, the age is 14–21 and it is located in the solar plexus. It governs mental and personal power issues. It is associated with the pancreas and the action of the liver, spleen, stomach, gall bladder and nervous system.

It is a time to be self-assertive and to have a sense of power and the courage to choose what you stand for. There are multiple influences and controls as you move into the business world; these include such things as bosses, coworkers, competition, media, technology and international connections.

Fourth Chakra

The colour is green, the age is 21–28 and the location is the heart. It is about transformation and love, is associated with the thymus gland and governs the heart, blood and circulatory system. It also influences the immune and endocrine systems.

The word "transformation" is the key at this level, because it is about moving into heart energy. This chakra is the middle point between the first three chakras of physical development and the next three chakras of insight and spirituality. Many of us just get to the level of the third chakra or business mentality and haven't allowed the heart to help us connect to higher aspects of ourselves.

Fifth Chakra

The colour is blue, the age is 28–35 and the location is the throat. It is associated with the thyroid gland and governs vocal cords, bronchial apparatus, lungs and metabolism.

This chakra is the centre for communication, expression, judgment and creativity. It is a time when you begin to find your own voice and speak your truth. Sound is a great healer and has connections to higher realms.

Sixth Chakra

The colour is indigo, the age is 35–42 and the location is the centre of the forehead; it is also known as the third eye. It is associated with the master pituitary gland and governs the lower brain, the nervous system, the ears, the nose and the left eye.

This chakra is the eye of the personality as we consider our spiritual nature. There is a hunger to experience the meaning of life and the ability to see the divine in all things. It's a knowingness beyond insight that connects with our deep-seated intuition, our soul. This is when the empty nesters begin to look for the answer to the question, "Who am I?"

Seventh Chakra

The colour is white, the age is ageless and the location is the crown, the top of our head. It is associated with the pineal gland and governs the upper brain and the right eye. It's pure, undifferentiated cosmic knowledge, a feeling of integration with God.

Body Symbology

Our body is the most intricate and complex organism on earth; it organizes cells, organs, glands and systems to communicate and work in harmonious teamwork to keep us alive and well. It has also created a way to speak with our personality through symbology, to tell us what we need to do to help the internal team keep us healthy.

As well as communication through the chakras with organs and glands, there are other parts of the body that give us messages about what is bothering or affecting us.

The following chart gives some examples of areas of the body and what they are symbolic of. You may become aware of others, and you can easily see on your own what they might signify. Based on location in the body, these parts also have a relationship with the seven chakras. Poorly functioning chakras can be picked up from energy work, as well as from their location and relationship to the physical.

When parts of your body are ill, uncomfortable or broken, the location of the problem speaks to what needs to be looked at on a deeper level. Pay attention to the chart below and see if any red flags pop up for you. If so, ask yourself if it is related to an imprint imposed by someone else, or if it is clearly yours.

It is important to pay attention to any discomfort in your body, acknowledge where it is coming from and *listen* to what message it is giving you. The chart will help you understand your body better.

Body Part	Symbolic Message
Eyes	What is it that you don't want to see?
Throat	How you communicate your truth, find your voice
Shoulders	Carrying burdens, the weight of the world
Arms	Hold and embrace experiences of life
Wrists	Movement and ease
Hands	Holding on, letting go
Heart	Centre of life, security, broken heart
Breasts	Nurturing, give too much, bitterness backs up
Lungs	Breath of life, freedom to change
Upper Back	Emotional, unloved
Middle Back	Get off my back
Lower Back	Fear of money, lack of support
Stomach	What can't you digest? Conflict
Liver	Congestion, seat of anger
Gall Bladder	Bitterness in life
Spleen	Immunity
Pancreas	Sweetness of life
Colon	Willingness to absorb
Bladder	Pissed off with something
Elimination	Holding on to or releasing stuff
Uterus	Sexual issues
Hips	Carries the body in balance
Joints	Flexibility, mobility, direction
Legs	What supports you, holds you up?
Knees	Flexibility, willingness to bend
Ankles	Connection to your foundation
Feet	Something to stand on, stepping forward

In my work as a holistic health practitioner, the first half hour of a session is listening to clients talk. They may not be clear about why they came to see me, but during the conversation I hear wording like, "I just can't stomach my new job," or "I feel like the weight of the world is on my shoulders." These words define what is happening, and if you listen closely to your own conversations, you will learn a lot. These words tell me what chakra area I will work on.

From the comments I hear, I am able to craft questions while the client is in an altered state on the therapy table, which helps to open a door for them to answer their own questions. People are amazed how buried answers come to the surface, and they ask, "Where did that come from?" Acknowledgement alone can begin the healing process; it's usually something they instinctively knew but just weren't listening to their body's messages.

The following are a couple of examples from my life. With the first one, I experienced a number major of gastrointestinal bleeds over several years, and they were trying to tell me about issues in my life that I couldn't stomach or digest. It took me a long time before I was willing to accept they were associated with relationship issues. In the meantime, my stomach was bleeding the life out of me, and it could have been fatal. The next one was an abusive relationship, where I was beaten up to the point that I couldn't see through my swollen eyes. The clue was I didn't want to see what was wrong with my life. Those messages are so clear to me now, but at the time I had no idea what body symbology was.

As you become more aware of the symbolic meaning of your body parts, you can ask your own questions; you'll see more about crafting the question in chapter 5. We must acknowledge and deal with these messages, or they will become a reality as the body continually hears your words. Comments I sometimes hear are, "That's just killing me," or "I'm dying to do such and such." When you begin to understand how your body speaks to you, you also need to be aware that the body also hears what you say and follows your orders. Be careful what you put out there. If you do not pay attention to body messages, then you are telling it *you* don't matter.

Once you understand body symbology, it offers literal messages that are fairly easy to understand. As you play with the meaning of each chakra and its associated glands and organs, it gives you insight about others. For example, gall bladder problems are associated with the third chakra and are about holding bitterness. To heal the problem, you have to pay attention to what you are bitter about and then take action to correct the issue.

Physical parts of the body have a job to do, and that gives you a clue about how they speak to you. For example, legs hold you up, carry you and support you. When they are not doing that job, ask yourself what is going on in your life that doesn't support you. This type of investigation can be like kids playing in kindergarten: light-hearted and fun. If you don't try too hard and don't take the game too seriously, the answers will come.

Some messages may be experienced in a subtle way, through issues and feelings. They can come to our awareness like dolphins popping up from the waves, but in a moment they are gone. Those moments are precious—pay special attention to their meaning when they continue to resurface.

Pain is more obvious. It is a loud emotion, and if you don't pay attention and truly listen to the message, it just gets louder. Emotional, physical and mental pain are all calling for attention. Learn how to read the messages from your body and take action to deal with the underlying cause.

Mental and emotional wounds aren't a punishment—they are an opening of opportunity. Think about how, when the body incurs a physical wound, it invokes resources such as white blood cells, adrenaline and energy to rush to the site to assist with healing. We can also learn to invoke our own healing mechanisms for emotional hurts by using intent and focus to call on our energy for help.

As mentioned earlier in this chapter, each chakra expands out into the auric field. The Inca shamans teach that everything that has happened to us (and will happen to us) sits in this field, and from here it can be healed before it penetrates the physical body and causes disease. When the body speaks to us, it can be through our own words, by what we sense through intuition or what we feel in our body. When something we haven't taken care of is still in our auric field, and we listen to our body messages, we have an opportunity to deal with and heal the issue before it affects our physical body.

As you move through the next section on acknowledgement, some feelings will surprise you. When dealing with issues that are sensitive, the most common result is to *react* rather than respond. We blow up, cry, feel sorry for ourselves or internalize and hold in strong emotions. Pay attention to the chart below and see how the chakras can help you process strong feelings: acknowledge the issue (1), stay with your senses and allow the initial strong feeling (2) to process through to an opinion (3) and then on to a second feeling in the heart centre (4). Now the throat (5) can give a logical response as you move to insight (6) that looks at the whole picture and then to release (7) through the crown. It becomes a productive cycle rather than a painful one. It takes some thoughtful time but is worth the result.

Chakra	Action
Seven (7)	Release
Six (6)	Insight
Five (5)	Response
Four (4)	Second feeling
Three (3)	Opinion
Two (2)	Feeling, reaction
One (1)	Concept, issue

When in alignment, the chakras process in a healthy manner. Make friends with your chakras—they can help you.

PART III

Finding Your Way Home

FOUR

Acknowledgement

*We have to be accountable for the life we live and be
connected with our source. To walk through the fog
of our cultural trance and recover from the multitude
of forces that surround us, we have to be willing to
change our perception and find our true reality.*
—James Hollis

THIS STEP IN THE process is more defining on a personal
level and will take work and commitment on your part. You
will work with charts that have just one word at a time to
consider; decide if it has meaning for you in any way, and if
so, does it have a hold on you? Has it imprinted your life?

Once you become aware of the stories other people have
created for you, you have an opportunity to investigate
further and understand if they are part of your truth. Do
the seeds that were planted in your psyche represent how
you truly feel about life, or are they a mixture of weeds and
wildflowers?

This investigative process requires clarity about what
speaks to your heart or what ruffles your feathers. Let your
intuitive self help you with the answers. When you ask

yourself such a question, your intuition is the first thought that comes to mind, before you analyze and judge it. Use this first thought.

Notes to Review before You Begin

The Largest Imprints Begin in the Family

In my own family, the atmosphere was warm, loving and happy. The music we played was country western, and we attended a community-oriented United Church. My parents were not highly educated and never thought of encouraging my sister and me to attend university.

Another scenario might be for the families of doctors and lawyers. Education to follow in the parents' footsteps would be promoted, and most likely classical music was played in the home. The religion may have been Catholic, and the atmosphere one of higher expectations.

This next example comes from the autobiography of a tennis champion, Andre Agassi, called *Open*. From the time Andre was a baby, his father had decided he would be a tennis champion. In his crib he had a ping pong paddle taped to his hand so he could bat balls in the mobile above him. As a child he spent all his free time in the backyard hitting tennis balls from a giant machine called "the dragon" that his father had created. In his book, Andre says, "My life has never for one day belonged to me ... My life has always belonged to someone else ... I learn about myself, created myself through imitation. How else could I do it?"

These three scenarios are just a few examples of how a family setting and upbringing sets the tone and imprints who we will become. They are deep because they begin at conception and continue through our growing and developing years.

Because history repeats itself, look at what part of your family history you carry forward to your present family situation. If your childhood was unhappy, decide what you want to replay and what to leave behind. "Let go and let God" is a motto I learned from the book *You Were Born Rich* by Bob Proctor, and as I made major transitions in my life, it served me well. You can release old issues to the universe once you become aware of them; it doesn't have to be difficult, and the universe doesn't judge. Remember, some imprints from your family come from race, culture and generational history, and you bring them forward into your present families. If such issues don't make you feel good, it's time to stop their perpetration into your children and following generations. If they are important to you, pass them on.

We all grow up in less than ideal circumstances and families—you are not alone. Issues in some families may be yelling, physical abuse and violence that cause children to retreat into their own world as they build barriers of protection to survive. Other families, with both parents working or that foster a sense of indifference towards the children, create a void for love and nurturing that definitely carries forward. This void can transcend into a need to fill the empty space with something or someone else, such as addictions or codependence. On another note, many imprints feel right and are exactly where you want to be. For these positive imprints, celebrate them and be thankful. Take time to enjoy their value and what you learned about yourself.

The topics on the charts are meant to be thought-provoking as you delve into your history and the developed patterns. Life is about lessons, so if everything was perfect from the beginning, we would all be in Nirvana right now. Also, remember perfection is in the eyes of the beholder, and it is different for each unique individual.

We can't relive the past and probably don't want to. What would be helpful at this point is to remember the feelings and experiences that made you happy, unhappy or confused. Did you want to be an artist but were directed to be a lawyer? Were you left-handed but forced to write with your right hand? Put some thought into who you are and who you are not. Use feelings, gut reactions and love in your thought processes as you move through this section.

Labels and Titles

Within all of these bosses and controls, there is another way by which people identify themselves. When asked who you are, you will most often reply with your name. Your identity also has multiple labels attached, such as mother, sister, daughter, cook, Catholic, recovering alcoholic, doctor, president and so on. We tend to label ourselves by what we do and not by who we truly are, our *being*. As you work through the charts, don't forget about the power of the labels. If you peeled them off, who would you be? Work with who is beneath the labels.

Step Out of the Story

The previous section about awareness gave you food for thought about various influences that may have moulded who you are. In this section on acknowledgement, it is time to become the detective and the investigator, but best of all the observer without attachment to the story. Acknowledgement of your stories and imprints is not about blame or judgment about who did what to whom. This exercise is about collecting information that created your present personality. Allow yourself to play with thoughts, options and opportunities; stay as impartial as possible while you review and remember. By remaining the unattached observer, you see things more clearly.

Does your memory come from an action, a sound, an image, a person or possibly some type of abuse? Did the issue become a secret, a reality that was enjoyable or scary? This is about you. Take your time to investigate thoroughly. You probably never looked at your life in such detail before. Some insights may come to you that you don't understand right now, but trust that they have value. As you move along in your search, the meaning will arrive, often when you least expect it.

In some cases we have built other stories around the past that can include barriers and fantasy. Thought processes and self-indulgent desires can create foregone conclusions of things that never really happened. Be aware that stories created in our mind are there to mask or fulfill something else, but the effects are real. Look for what is under the mask.

The invitation to the reader is to identify what is not truly yours or what no longer fits, if it ever did. Through this process of identification, some issues may simply flake away like dead skin after a sunburn. Other areas will take more work and time to shed as you reprogram and edit your personal belief system. The exciting part is for every ending, there is a new beginning waiting through the door of opportunity. You'll find more clarity and lightness as you move forward, one step at a time. The important part is your willingness to use intuition and discernment to determine what fits for you and what does not.

Through the process of acknowledgement, stay unattached to the personal with the use of symbolic tools. For example, you can visualize the imprints and patterns you recognize as layers of clothing you've added to keep you comfortable and safe. As you peel them off, you will feel the heaviness, which you have carried for a long time, reduce. You will feel lighter and freer as you eventually reach the purity of your own skin that has been well masked with barriers of protection. You may not be able to shed all embedded imprints, but you can learn how to recognize them for what they are and how they influence you.

The Investigative Process

We are a stranger to ourselves in many ways. Life can catch us in an illusion, such as the need for a certain person's approval to shape our character, integrity and honesty. We need to muster the courage to detach from that need. Our world will change when we shatter this illusion, and we will have to be ready to find the strength and willingness to step out and find our own way. This search will evolve piece by piece as we set our intent to unravel the mystery of our lives.

As you move deeper into the process of investigation, take stock of the patterns, imprints and influences you recognize as part of you, and put them in categories. Some will work well in groups if they relate to others. When the initial ones are dealt with, others may fall away naturally. It is also good to rate them with what sense of urgency they carry; then begin to work with the most important ones first.

When deciding what does not serve you, pay attention

to how the boss affected you; look at it from many angles and directions. Where did it come from, and who was the influence? If your awareness causes you to change, how will the outcome affect you? What difference will it make to your life and those around you? Will it release you from imprisoning habits and bring you comfort with an "ah ha" sense of relief? This exercise is not just a mental game but must include all your senses and feelings for you to embody the change. Be prepared for the outcome.

We need to own some of our reality, and in doing so we will find the reason issues have tracked us through life. For instance, if we are negative, we attract negativity. Where did it begin? Is it from family habits or embedded fear, or is it from anger and fear created by our own thoughts? When we recognize where it comes from, we can release ourselves from the source by installing a new core belief in opposition to what we presently hold. As we acknowledge and are willing to release the old beliefs, we create space energetically for new possibilities, direction and opportunity.

For many of us, there will be deeply imprinted issues that cause pain—emotionally, mentally and physically. They have been with us a long time, and when we meet with the same energy at times in our lives, it can trigger a response, often unknowingly, that causes us to react to old stories. Examples of such issues could be

- financial stress and discord;
- abuse of any kind;
- religious or racial issues;
- abandonment; and
- feelings of inadequacy.

Once you recognize the issues and your reaction to them, you have an opportunity to deal with them. You have a choice to stay in the power of the present moment as you acknowledge and release their hold on you. This will take practice and time, but like riding a bucking bronco, you will eventually bring it to submission.

Using the Charts

In the following pages there are charts with examples of influences and controllers that may have participated in forming your present personality. Some will be relevant, and I'm sure you will think of others that are also important to you. It's time to play and evaluate various options to get a sense of how some of these topics had an effect on you. There is no right or wrong. This process is about you, as a unique individual, uncovering aspects of your development as you determine by whom and how you were influenced. Think about which of them are false idols and which ones are the real and meaningful to you. You are here now because it's time to do your own work, so enjoy this journey of self discovery.

To keep issues in perspective, I have split the charts into two categories: "People and Things" and "Senses and Feelings." They are sorted alphabetically, not by any kind of rating. Additional charts can be downloaded from my website. The address is the back of the book.

The charts contain *words* and words carry images, that will help you remember your story. Sit with them, daydream, write about them and leave space for more reflections that will surface. You may want to use a journal to record what you find. Pay attention to emotions or feelings associated with various scenarios and make a note of them.

It will be easy to just glance at the various topics and brush them off because you don't think they relate to you. Slow down and mull each one over so you don't miss something that is simmering below the surface. Even if that topic has no meaning, it may register something else that is similar. If you have chosen to read this book, it's important to you, so make sure not to miss something important.

People and Things

Alcohol	
Bullying	
Cell phones	
Children	
Coworkers	
Colleagues	
Computer / Games	
Doctors	
Drugs	
Education	
E-mailing / Texting	
Employer	
Gambling	
Gangs	
Genetics	
Government	
Laws	
Magazines	
Management	
Marriage	

People and Things

Media	
Medical System	
Money / Credit Cards	
Name	
Parents	
Police / Judicial	
Politics	
Race	
Relationship	
Religion	
Rules	
Siblings	
Social Media	
Society	
Spouse	
Students / Friends	
Teachers / Mentors	
Technology	
Television	
Work	

Senses and Feelings

Anger	
Anxiety	
Body Image	
Broken Heart	
Change	
Codependency	
Communication	
Death	
Diets	
Ego	
Envy	
Expectations	
Failure	
Fear	
Frustration	
Grief	
Guilt	
Hopelessness	
Illness / Pain	
Inner Critic	

Senses and Feelings

Irritation	
Jealousy	
Judgment	
Loneliness	
Mind Chatter	
Negativity	
Sadness	
Secrets / Lies	
Security / Safety	
Self -Esteem	
Skepticism	
Social Image	
Stress	
Stupid	
The Truth	
Trapped	
Unloved	
Unworthy	
Worry	

You Are the Boss of You

Now that you've checked in with your psyche and asked yourself some gut-wrenching questions, do you feel like you are on one of the *Survivor* shows, or are you busting with the pride of an *American Idol*?

As a society, we have been waiting for a long time for someone else to fix us, to rescue us, to tell our fortune and to draw us a road map for our life's journey. It's time to stop and find this road ourselves. We are on the right path, so we shouldn't give up.

It took time for the overlays to be embedded in you, and you won't recognize and release them all at once, but each time a new awareness surfaces and you acknowledge where it came from, you have the choice to disable its power. You might have to recognize it again and again, but it will disappear. It is a habit you need to break.

These ideas may sound farfetched, but even if you just acknowledged some of the imprints and bosses that have created your identity, you'll understand your present personality has been a visitor in disguise.

There are many world disasters happening with greater frequency, and everyone holds some responsibility for these occurrences. We all carry a piece to this never-ending puzzle, and we have to take charge of ourselves first and foremost in order to make a difference for the world and future generations.

Blaming others for who you are doesn't hold water, and the past is just that—the past. The only way to change is to take control of yourself and be willing to move forward, with your heart as your guide. The puck stops at your own front door, and you are the only one with a key to open that door to your authentic self.

PART IV

Call Off the Search—
You Are Already There

FIVE

Be the Choreographer of Your Life

When things become very clear about who you are, reality
shifts and things that were important no longer matter.
—Jean Houston

THIS LAST STEP WAS going to include tools and exercises, but
if you have worked through the first part of the book, you are
far beyond the need for that. You already know somewhere
in your gut that you are ready for change and are willing
to take action. When I asked *I Ching,* a book of ancient
Chinese wisdom and system of changes, what was needed
here, the advice I was given was, "Casual talk in informal
surroundings can restore confidence."

You won't be sitting in meditation or writing out positive
sayings a hundred times. Instead, we will share stories and
insights that may resonate with what you've been uncovering
in the last few chapters. Deep down, you are the only one
who truly knows your *authentic self,* so in the end you are
the only one who can rewrite your story. I can't tell you
which parts to change, but I can offer you guidance, wisdom
and advice from various meaningful sources. They may help

ignite some of your creative resources. There is magic in everything—take hold of it and let it work for you.

Crafting the Question

You'll notice there are many questions in this book that I leave open-ended for you to answer. I do that because you alone know your own answers, your own truth. One of the hurdles you face in this section, and ultimately in your life, is how to craft your own questions that will help you find answers. You cannot get the right answer if you fail to ask the right question.

In my holistic health practice, crafting the question is a basis for most treatments I use. Initially, through dialogue with clients I listen to what they have to say about why they came for a treatment. Their reason is often only part of the story. Additional words spoken as miscellaneous chatter about other issues or people are often more meaningful and lead to the source of the problem. While on the therapy table, I rephrase their own comments into questions and ask them to answer with the first thought that comes to them (called intuition). People are amazed and surprised at what pops out, because it is something they already knew subliminally but hadn't validated.

You are able to illicit a true response that is yours alone if you pay attention to your gut response, your intuition and your soul. Intuition is a valuable tool; it's all-knowing, beyond your mind and ego. The biggest challenge is to allow, learn and trust what comes to you. When you don't know what to do, or think you don't know, consider this example. Imagine drinking a glass of milk that has turned sour; you immediately know it is bad. It's a quick sense or a gut reaction. Follow the same idea with other happenings in your life, and pay attention to your gut reaction and your first response.

Intuition has always been there, but we have been programmed to use the answers of others and take them on as our own. We have been ordered around and told what to do for so long that we have lost the use of our intuitive senses, which hold our own answers. As you become aware and attentive to how and when others have answered your questions, you have the choice to take your voice back.

As you move through life experiences, rather than react to emotion, slow down and craft yourself a question to find out if the issue represents your highest good. Then learn to pay attention and listen to your intuitive response. If you continue to ask others what you should do, you are giving away your power. Answer the question yourself, and you'll be amazed how good it will make you feel as you move from being under an amorphous shadow to a place of clarity, focus and power. Knowledge is what you've learned, and wisdom is how wisely you choose to use the knowledge you have attained. Remember, this wisdom is yours, so honour it. Take a risk, act for yourself and speak your truth as you move away from the opinions of others.

Be as One

If asked on a job application about your level of spirituality, how would you define yourself? Would you use a label of Catholic, Muslim, Christian, Jehovah's Witness or other, or would you talk about things like love, truth, your connection to nature, helping others, meditation, peace and joy?

Remember the words from Shirley MacLaine's book: "Religions teach religion, not spirituality." Your heart is always there to guide you in the direction of spirituality.

It's when you make friends with your soul that you become who you truly are. Your authentic personality is your soul's message—your life purpose. When your personality is your soul and your soul is your personality, you become one with yourself and with the universe.

Our guide on my recent trip to Egypt was always calling us together to "be as one." Depending on our location or his tone of voice, I would hear the message differently. Sometimes it was about bringing our group together physically, but other times it was about being one with ourselves, being fully present in the moment, being one with our surroundings or being one with the history of the temple or pyramid we were visiting.

However it feels for you, the saying "Be as one" is a useful guide for you to focus on as you pull together all of your own unique pieces of the oneness of your being on this journey of self-discovery. In this search for your true, authentic self, as you remove the imprints and stories others have created for you, you will be able to define who you are with certainty and honesty.

Once you know your true self, you will find there is no difference between you and your neighbours. Your authentic self is the deep truth of knowingness that we are all love; it's oneness and unity. We may have differences of opinion, race and background, but that offers variety and creative thinking. If you stay locked into the consciousness of "My way is the only way," the creativity stops and you are stuck in criticism and discord.

By shedding your outdated programs, belief systems and

masks, you have the opportunity to think globally. Making a shift in yourself has an impact on the collective, and in this changing world, it's time to broaden your personal views to include the collective and *be as one.*

Labyrinth versus Maze

The labyrinth is a single, spiral path created for people to walk in a meditative state as a spiritual journey, whereas a maze relates to a garden of dead ends and decisions that create confusion and chaos.

The labyrinth, according to *Walking a Sacred Path* by Dr. Lauren Artress, is "an ancient, mystical tool that can help prepare ourselves for 'transformation of the human personality in progress' and accomplish a 'shift in consciousness' as we seek spiritual maturity as a species. We are called to do nothing less."[4] This next quote about mazes is taken from *Labyrinths: Walking Toward the Center* by Gernot Candolini. "If life is a maze, every mistake is an unnecessary detour and a waste of time. If life is a labyrinth, then every mistake is part of the path and an indispensable master teacher."[5]

People have often confused the two entities as being the same, but their meanings are significantly different. We see corn mazes in many places in the fall of the year, and often large gardens are designed as a maze but are chaotic in nature with no spiritual meaning. On the other hand, the labyrinth has one single path leading into the centre and out again. It offers a powerful meditative value as the person sheds what doesn't serve him or her on the way in, and it provides a

4   Lauren Artress. *Walking a Sacred Path*, New York: The Berkley Publishing Co., 1995.
5   Candolini, Gernot. *Labyrinths: Walking Toward the Center*, The Crossroads Publishing Company, 2003.

centre to pause, reflect and refocus before walking back out with clarity for new beginnings.

Do you live your life in a maze often lost and bumping into dead ends full of frustration and chaos? Is this because you are not clear on the picture of who you truly are? Are you trying to walk a path that follows in others' footsteps—where the agenda is different and the shoes don't fit? If so, stop and clean out the spiritual and physical closets full of burdens, including the word *should*. Start walking a path that is your own—one that brings you pleasure and happiness as you connect with your inner spirit. Move from the maze of confusion to the sacred labyrinth. The shedding is mainly psychological but may also include some material values that weigh you down and cause you stress.

The Worry Chart (from the book *Three Boxes of Life*)

I have carried this chart, written on a piece of paper, with me for years. I also have a small box of worry dolls that can be used to talk to, discuss the worry and then put them back in the box where they belong. They are still there if I want to revisit them, but while in the box they lose their power and control over me.

Contents of the Worry Chart:

- Forty percent will never happen.
- Thirty percent has already happened (reminds you how much you have changed).
- Twelve percent is about your health or someone else's.
- Ten percent is petty/miscellaneous.

- Eight percent is real; half we can't change, and half we can act on.

If it's real and you can act on it, do so; otherwise, let go of the unnecessary, stressful burden.

Shape Shifting

A recent e-mail that circulated several times was about not what you say, but how you say it. A blind man collecting money on the street was receiving very little, when a young woman came along and looked at his sign that said, "I am blind and need money." She rewrote the sign to say, "It's a beautiful day—but I can't see it." Immediately people became more generous with their donations.

Change your words and thoughts, and you change your world. Shift the shape of an experience and change your perception. No object or person is a mystery; the mystery is how you look at things.

An example of this for me was learning to change my perception of the outside world when it was night and dark. It was a fearful place for me, because as a child I had been told the dark was full of bad and dangerous people—like bogeymen. When we built our cottage in the Gulf Islands, I was often there alone, and in the winter it got dark early. I still had to walk the dog, the stars were beautiful in a clear sky and I wanted to enjoy them. I began to rethink about the beauty of the dark, so I started by standing just outside the front door and then gradually moved onto the porch. As days and weeks went on, I became more comfortable outside at night. I was careful and carried a flashlight and cell phone, but I was no longer fearful. I changed my perception of the dark, and it has been a wondrous experience. We now have our retirement home on the island, with no curtains on the windows. Dark is now a total non-issue for me. Change often takes time because our minds and bodies are conditioned to what we are used to, but it certainly is not impossible to change, and the newfound freedom is powerful.

Shedding and Releasing

The words in the heading have been used throughout the book and can vary from simple and immediate items to more complex and time-consuming issues. Either way, if you want to get rid of things, you have to take it seriously and include the soul in your decision. To make the release meaningful and carry weight, it is helpful to use symbolic and physical gestures that the body understands. Some examples would be writing the issues out on paper that you crumple up and throw away or burn in a fire. You can also speak about the issue into a stick, a stone or another piece of nature, and then throw it into the water or a fire. These are simple actions, but they have powerful symbolic and energetic meaning to the body and soul. Depending on the severity of the issue, you may have to repeat the process a number of times. All of these actions lighten our burdens and the needless weight we carry.

A simple action of shedding materials happened for me when we built our home on the island. It took several years to build our home, and many of our things remained in boxes all that time. When it was time to move into the house, I had forgotten what was in a number of boxes, and I had never missed any of it. I packed the boxes in the trunk of the car and took them to a fundraising garage sale, donating all of them without looking back. The action was meaningful and definitely carried weight, and I was happy to shed what I certainly didn't need.

The type of issue that takes more work to release is a deep imprint or label from childhood that is repeatedly reinforced, such as "Your are so stupid," or "You'll always be fat." No matter what people do to change this perception, they still believe the imprint is true. The result may cause actions such as anorexia or bulimia because the belief is so ingrained. These types of imprints need to be dealt with in layers, as you acknowledge and work with the issue each time it arises. When the emotion involved makes you feel bad, stop right then and pay attention to what pictures, thoughts and senses surface for you. Play at reversing the picture or picking yourself out of the picture. This is also called shape shifting, as discussed above, and it has been used historically by medicine men to remove evil spirits and disease at a symbolic level. As you play with changing the picture of your perception, you are rewriting the story of who you are. You may also need assistance from other practitioners from time to time.

Under this heading of releasing and shedding, I have given examples from the simple to very difficult. Most other things would fit somewhere in between, but the theory of using symbology helps the body and soul understand that you want to make a change. The time needed to shed and change will vary with each individual and imprint. Trust that you matter, that your life has meaning and that you have the right to be true to you and you alone. It's a journey of love for yourself and those who follow you.

Activation

To activate is to start a process, and in this case, it is about finding your voice in the world. We are part of a rapidly changing world, and technology has sped it up for us. As we move to a higher level of vibration, consciousness and oneness, it is time for us to take charge of our true essence and help others to do the same. As you shed the cocoon that binds you, be willing to release your control over others. Replace ego and power issues with love and unity, as you activate your soul to live in a more harmonious space.

I recently returned from Egypt, where the country had gone through a revolution from January 25 to February 11, 2011, and the people were just beginning to live in a new world of freedom. They welcomed us with open arms and a happiness that was inspiring to every one of us. We were a group of 34 travelling as "spiritual pilgrims" to help reactivate the light for everyone and everything, including the ancient temples of our history.

It is time for all of us to be an active player in our lives, just as these Egyptians were, and to stand up for what is right. Be a system buster and take your life back from one entrenched and controlled by the imprints and patterns of others. It will take time and patience, but the choice to act is the beginning of your new found celebration of freedom. Call on the spirit of Egypt for help and believe you also can make a change.

We are all part of the worldwide web, and everything we do affects and makes a difference to the web of wholeness for all. We tend to detach ourselves from issues if they are painful, but if we stow them inside and walk away, they fester within and affect our health, our soul and our place in the world.

The people of Egypt had become complacent and were sleepwalking robots to a power-hungry president. Most of them had never voted during their lifetime because they took for granted that they had no choice. After the revolution, 85 percent of the population lined the streets to vote on the referendum about their new direction. The results were 77 percent "yes" for freedom.

The day after the vote, our bus was in the centre of the famed Tahrir Square, surrounded with crowds of people. They were so happy as they waved to us with peace signs, and we responded in the same manner. It was a powerful feeling to be part of their celebration. Their unwinding of old ways will take many trials of testing to find the right balance, but we all have to begin somewhere, and the choice to change is the first step in the activation of each new journey. Their action to be free speaks to the whole world as well as to each individual. It makes us aware that we all count and that we all have a voice in the world.

Removing the Mask

On our Egyptian trip, our spiritual group also visited the Temple of Dier el Bahari, the home of Pharaoh Hatchepsut. During that time, pharaohs had to be male heirs from the female bloodline. Hatchepsut did not have sons to inherit the throne, so she assumed the position of pharaoh. She dressed as a male and portrayed the role of a powerful person. She lived behind a mask for her entire reign.

We arrived right after the revolution, and there were no other tourists, so our spiritual group was able to experience a ceremony to honour Goddess Hatchepsut. She channelled messages to us through our leader, Aluna Joy, and told us we had to remove our masks, like the one she had worn as pharaoh. She said it was time for all of us to shed the masks of the past and to walk in the light, to be authentic and transparent.

As we stood in a circle and received her messages, Aluna Joy asked, "Okay, that sounds great to become unmasked, to be more authentic, but what are the ramifications?" The answer was, "You are going to feel vulnerable, because you are stepping into new territory. You are going to open up and let something inside of you out that you never let anyone see before."

Her message was for the world, so you can see you are not alone in your journey of shedding masks and the baggage of the past. It may not be easy, but it will be worth it.

Where Do You Go from Here?

Each step of change is about how you enjoy the journey without attachment to the outcome, because that may change as you begin to see things more clearly. You need to be heard and should focus on how to express yourselves, instead of what the issue is about. Without such criteria and barricades, we allow change to flow more freely in a direction that is for the highest good of all.

As Stephen Levine says in *Turning toward the Mystery*, "Our world is neutered by interpretation." We all see things through the filters we are imprinted with throughout life. We need to remove these filters and veils that cloud our perception of what reality truly is. Finding our way home to our soul, our authentic self, is a challenge and takes work, but it is also a gift of pride and compassion you give yourself.

There are many spiritual teachings about soul-searching at a deeper level than what we are talking about here. This book is merely a simple awakening about how many of your thoughts and values are not truly yours, and once you shed them and lighten the load, your clarity and perception of life will be greatly enhanced. From there you can move forward to more teachings or just experience life through the purity of your own eyes and heart. You can call off the search of who you are because you are already there.

Write a new, honest story about yourself, and as Denise Cunningham says in *Whispers of Hope*, let the story of you be ennobling and one of grandeur. You have learned so much about who you are and who you are not, so it will be a playful journey filled with gratitude and love. Self-trust is a major step forward, and imagination is the highest kite that can fly if you allow it to take flight. As you move through the maze of contradiction that has surrounded you in the past, you will *become* the clarity and light you truly are.

BY PERMISSION OF RICK DETORIE AND CREATORS SYNDICATE, INC.

Like this cartoon from *One Big Happy*, the last pages are blank. It is not a rip-off, just an open invitation to rewrite your life story. This book belongs to you.

Sincerely,
Alma C. Lightbody

Journal Notes

Journal Notes

Journal Notes

Journal Notes ————————————————

Journal Notes ————————————————

Journal Notes

Journal Notes

Journal Notes

Journal Notes ─────────────

Journal Notes

Journal Notes

Journal Notes

Journal Notes

Journal Notes

Journal Notes

Journal Notes

Acknowledgements

I want to acknowledge all my teachers, as well as my sisters of the sacred circles I am part of. The love and insight of all of them have been a major catalyst in my spiritual growth. I want to thank Erin Higgins, a client and friend, who passed her journals on to me to share her story, called *My Wonderful Nightmare*. The experience from writing that book gave me the incentive to complete this book, whose ideas have been tumbling around in my head for almost 10 years.

My gratitude also goes to my husband, Mack, who supports anything I choose to do, without question. He has encouraged my travel far and wide for teachings and adventures in many places including Peru, Egypt and Canyon de Chelley.

At this point, I want to state that the opinions in this book are mine even though they have been greatly influenced by all my teachers, clients and life experiences. I have always kept journals and binders full of information that I felt was important. Unfortunately, in the early years I sometimes didn't keep note of where some of the jewels of wisdom came from. To all of you I have not acknowledged, my sincere gratitude.

About the Author

Alma C. Lightbody, born in 1945 in Saskatchewan, Canada, is the youngest of two daughters.

She has degrees in medical technology, an MBA in business, experience in sales and multiple certificates in management, holistic health and shamanic healing. For the last 20 years she has focused on energy medicine. Her training, life experiences and work with clients has generated an awareness of the soul wisdom that needs to be shared with the world. She is coauthor of *My Wonderful Nightmare*.

Alma enjoys golfing and volunteer work and lives with her husband, Mack, in a home on the waterfront of Pender Island, British Columbia, Canada.

Find me on my website: www.almalightbody.com